Inspirational RELIGIOUS POEMS

WORDS OF ENCOURAGEMENT

BY IDA PEARL WEST CANADY

Copyright © 2014 by Ida Pearl West Canady

Inspirational Religious Poems
Words of encouragement
by Ida Pearl West Canady

Printed in the United States of America

ISBN 9781498406017

All rights reserved solely by the author. The author guarantees all contents are original and do not infringe upon the legal rights of any other person or work. No part of this book may be reproduced in any form without the permission of the author. The views expressed in this book are not necessarily those of the publisher.

Scripture quotations taken from the King James Version (KJV) – *public domain*

www.xulonpress.com

BIOGRAPHY

I was born in Centerville, Texas in 1950; I am the tenth child of twelve children born to Hosie and Zetha West. My parents were a great inspiration to me; I admired the missionary work they did in my hometown. They were God-fearing parents.

While in High School I accepted Jesus as my personal Savior. After graduation, I moved to Fort Worth, Texas where many of my brothers and sisters lived. Two years later I married my husband Hubert Canady at the Good Hope Missionary Baptist Church on the south side of Fort Worth, Texas under the founder and leadership of Pastor Rayford Thompson, where we were members for forty years in which he pastored for thirty-eight. I was a teacher of Sunday school for twenty-six years also served in many other fields. Pastor Rayford Thompson retired as pastor and passed the leadership on to Pastor Donald Horton. After going to several funerals at Great Commission and hearing Pastor Brown preach, we were eager to hear more of his teaching so we went to several Wednesday night Bible studies and we became members of the Great Commission Baptist Church Pastor/Teacher Douglass E. Brown (CEF). I completed my Level 1 course in Children's Evangelism Fellowship, which Great Commission Baptist Church sponsored me. This enabled me to teach the word of God in a after school program (Good News Club). I am also a member of the Evangelism Team, where we go out in many neighborhoods compelling others to accept Jesus Christ as their personal Savior.

My husband and I are the proud parents of four children; three sons Sheldon, Neoko and Kenneth, one daughter Sharon Washington, son in law Derrick Washington. We also have eight wonderful grandchildren and one great grandson. My husband Hubert and I have been married for almost forty-four years; he was a self-employed carpenter for over ten years and we have been the owners of A-1 Cleaning Service since 1995.

I received my certified Nurse's Assistant Certificate in 2007. I started writing in 1985, unfortunately I lost my manuscript did not realize until 2007 God was calling me to write inspirational poems.

Being encouraged by my husband, children, brothers, sisters and friends, I was inspired to publish my poems. These poems were written to leave a legacy for my family and their families and to encourage others.

I pray that these poems be an inspiration to someone and that someone's life will be blessed, changed, and challenged.

GRATITUDE

I am mighty grateful to God for his Love and Kindness, I can surely say that the Lord is good, His mercy is everlasting, and His truth endures to all generation.

I am thankful to my editor, my Christian friend Michelle Chambers for her patience, her kindness and her time—Michelle you truly have been there for me.

To the Xulon Publishing Company, you are one of a kind. Of all of the people you have worked with and published you took so much time and interest in me; I thank God for you.

To everyone that helped to make this happen—thank you.

—Ida Pearl West Canady

TABLE OF CONTENTS

God, Our Father 9
Black History 10
A New Stage in Life 11
Mother and Daughter Bond 12
Bride and Groom 13
Wonder Working God 14
Bless His Name 15
Another Chance 16
Alpha and Omega 17
Almighty God 18
Wonderful Savior 19
With Jesus' Stripes, We Are Healed 20
What a Change 21
We Need the Lord 22
We Didn't Come to Stay 23
Unlimited Rewards 24
Trials 25
The Word of God 26
The Son of God 27
Sacrifice 28
Missionaries for Christ 29
Christmas Time 30
The Lord, Our Guide 31
The Holy Spirit 32
Thank You, Lord 33
Savior 34
Praises 35
Pilgrims Traveling Through 36

Peace	37
No Pain No Gain	38
Jesus, the Savior of the World	39
Jesus is the Answer	40
I've Been Changed	41
Jesus is a Friend	42
Hallelujah	43
Great Is His Name	44
God's Love	45
God Sent His Son	46
God Knows All	47
Earthly Vessels	48
Fix It Jesus	49
Faith	50
Come to Jesus	51
Victorious	52
Walk Worthy	53
True Love	54
Undying Love	55
Survivor	56
Seek and Ye Shall Find	57
Redeem	58
Prayer	59
POWER	60
Not My Will Lord	61
Mother's Love	62
Meditate	63
Lord Over Long Term Illness	64
Led by the Spirit of God	65
I Worship Thee Lord	66
How Precious is His Name	67
Grace and Mercy	68
A Gift	69
God Created Man	70
Elderly	71
Dear Lord	72
Celebrate!!!	73
Building God's kingdom	74

God, Our Father

God sent His only Son to die for us
In Him, I put my trust
I was sinking deep in sin
But Jesus saved me and took me in
His ways are totally different from mine
Wherever He leads me is right all the time
A Shepherd watches over his flock
This is a job that never stops
A father guides and directs
Because we are His very elect

Black History

Dr. Martin Luther King had a dream that we all come together as one
God made that possible by giving up His only Son,
In a book called, The Making of a Mind, Dr. King's life informed
But in Romans 10:9, the word of God transforms
There was a born slave by the name of Callie House, the former slave struggled for ex-slaves reparations
What a blessing, but without Jesus in our life it's still a devastation
There was the event of Rosa Parks getting on the bus at Court Square Stop
Thanks be to God for all of this because it does mean a lot
These are records of things that happened in the past
But only what they did for Christ will last

A New Stage in Life

Please Lord, hear my plea
I need you to watch over me
I am going through a new stage in life
I know you know because You are all wise
With humility and truth it will help me in my youth
Realizing I will grow as I go
But only you can help make it so
Help me to take the bitter with the sweet
Knowing that's what makes your children so unique
I know across the land and sea
You can still watch over me
Help me glow, grow and go
Being mindful I must help to make it so
Going through this new stage I know
That you deserve more praise than we show
You are the beginning and the end from the rising of the sun to the going down of the same
Praise ye the Lord and bless His holy name

Mother and Daughter Bond

A mother and her daughter can have a bond
You can get serious and you can have fun
There is a knot you can't untie
It's a noble mother's example that God desired
Mothers, we must set the example for our daughters today
Teach them to love their husband and obey
Teach them that their children are a blessing indeed
This is by far the best seed
Let them know the value of a virtuous wife
And the differences it will make in their life
Ladies the fear of the Lord in our life should show
This can be seen by others you know
If we only trust and obey
I guarantee you God will show us the way

Bride and Groom

Jesus said I am the bride you are the groom
If you believe and obey you will be with me soon
I left you to tarry for a while
So continue to keep your smile
You are only a pilgrim in a barren land
You must know this, you must understand
I went away to prepare a place for you
I will come back so be true
Let not your Heart be troubled
Even though there will be struggles
It's only for a short while so keep the faith and continue to strive
Blessed assurance you are mine
Beyond the clouds, the sun still shines

Wonder Working God

He is the wonder working God
He is the bright and morning star
He is the lily of the valleys
He is everywhere you are

Bless His Name

Bless the name of Jesus, His love remains the same
Today, tomorrow, forevermore He doesn't ever change
He is a blessing to our hearts, young and old
Being sent by God to save our souls
The Holy Spirit touched our hearts and said to us this day
God is a Holy God, Jesus is the way

Another Chance

We have sinned and come short of God's glory
But we have been given another chance to tell His story
To tell a dying world that He sent His Son to die but He rose again
That we might live and be redeemed of our sins
He hung bled and died out on Calvary
That you and I might be free
God is an awesome God let us praise Him for another start
God all mighty is worthy of praise
He's our creator and He saves
Satan came to kill steal and destroy
But God said no one can take away my children's joy
He said my love will abide always If you abide in Me,
and My words abide in you, you will ask what you desire John 15:7
As sinners we were sinking deep in sin until we open our hearts
and allow Jesus to come in

Alpha and Omega

Jesus is the beginning and He is the end
He knows all about us and our sins
He's our Maker and Creator
He died for us He's our Savior
He know us better than we know ourselves
Even if there are things we don't want to tell
He created us with His purpose in mind
So He will be able to guide us just fine

Almighty God

He is our Lord and our God
Whatever problem you have He can solve
He is a problem solver and a way maker
If you trust Him and not be shaken
Satan came to deceive us
But God sent His Son to receive us
Jesus is the light of the world
And what a mighty God we serve

Wonderful Savior

He is the Savior of the world the one and only one to serve
He came that we might have life
All we have to do is let Him abide
He has great love for us all
He just wants us to trust and stand tall
Step out on faith without a shadow or a doubt
And know He is there to bring us out
Hold steadfast and don't waiver
He is the Son of God, our Savior
What a wonderful Savior He is
He gave His life that we may live

With Jesus' Stripes, We Are Healed

Surely He hath borne our grief and carried our sorrows Isaiah 53:4
He has been our Help in ages past and our hope for tomorrow
He was wounded for our transgressions Isaiah 53:5
There was also affliction and oppression
He was bruised for our iniquities Isaiah 53:5
For us specifically
With His stripes we are Healed Isaiah 53:5
He showed this special love out on Golgotha's Hill

What a Change

Saul was on a mission for Satan
But on the Damascus road His life was straightened
He was saved and sanctified
After himself, he denied
He proved He was worthy of His calling
Jesus wants to keep us all from falling
Just trust Him and obey
He will surely show us the way

We Need the Lord

We need the Lord every hour, every day
Guide our footsteps every step of the way
Lord, if we stumble if we fall
Pick us up and help us stand tall
We are weak but Thou are mighty
Help us to be strong and keep striving
The bible says the race is not to the swift, nor the battle to the strong
Lord we know when You are with us we can't go wrong
Eccl. 9:11

We Didn't Come to Stay

Don't put off tomorrow what you can do today
We are just pilgrims in a barren land we didn't come to stay
You may say there's trouble on every hand
Jesus knows, He understands
Trust Him and your needs He will supply
And you will be with Him in Heaven by and by

Unlimited Rewards

Jesus is your first life line
He is one of a kind
There is no need for a second
He paid the price and reckoned
There is no price He wouldn't pay
Beaten and scarred for you that day
Trust Him and be rewarded
All you have to do is get started
There is no limit to what He can do
Just come to Him and be true
Life is sweet and life is good
Even though we don't do all we should
He is the beginning, He is the end
Come to Him, He will wash away your sins
He is the Son of the living God no one can do a better job

Trials

Don't be disturbed or surprised when you go through trials
Looking at the problems you'll be distressed
But looking at Christ you'll be at rest
Problems were created to make us strong
So we wouldn't depend on our own
Focus your mind on Calvary
Jesus will work it out you'll see
Jesus is our Maker and our Creator
He is our Lord and our Savior

The Word of God

The word of God is pure
The word of God shall stand for ever
The word of God is quick and powerful
The word of God is sharper than any sword
His name is called word of God Rev 19:13

The Son of God

Jesus Christ is the Son of God He bore our sins
and gave us a new start
He's the reason we live today
It's a debt we cannot repay

Sacrifice

Because of Jesus Christ's sacrifice
It gave us an opportunity to be with Him in paradise
God so loved the world He gave His only begotten Son
This makes us a family of one
We are the family of the household of faith
Come everyone let us celebrate!!!

Missionaries for Christ

Missionaries are born not made
First of all you must be saved
You must have your weapon of life
Which only comes from Jesus Christ
Jesus calls us not only to come
But He also prepares us for the storm
David was a man after God's own heart
That comes from setting himself apart
Self promotion and servanthood don't mix
It's just one of Satan's little tricks
He will have us acting to impress
And dressing for success
But if you want your life to have impact
Tell a dying world the facts
Jesus is the Son of God
There is no problem He can't solve
He intercedes on our behalf
He had done this in ages past
He is our hope for years to come
This is for everyone not just for some
Jesus died for our sins
Now our mission is to help bring others in

Christmas Time

Christmas time is the time we see signs
The following year we start getting behind
Our faith starts wavering and signs disappear
But Jesus said I will be with you don't you fear
Take the time to be kind one to another
It will not cost you a dime nor any trouble
Jesus was born in a stable what a labor
But the signs the wise men saw was not a fable
He was born for our sins so that we may be washed and cleansed
Let us not forget it's not about us but it's all about Him

The Lord, Our Guide

Please Lord, lead us and direct us, don't let us go astray
Help us to be faithful, show us the right way
Prop us up on every side, don't let us slip nor slide
You were there
for the Israelites You were a cloud by day and a pillar of fire
by night
This lets us know You have all power and You are alright

The Holy Spirit

Where the spirit of the Lord is there is liberty
Looking forward to the ministry of Jesus Christ,
the Holy Spirit, inspired Isaiah to prophecy
Jesus said He would not leave us alone
He would send His Comforter to keep us strong
It's by the Holy Spirit that one confesses
That Jesus is Lord and He is the best

Thank You, Lord

Thank you Lord for your joy and peace
Without you where would we be
You are the answer to our prayer
Your grace and mercy have taught us to share
To share with others the good news
Letting them know you are the truth
You are a wonder working God,
thank you for coming into our hearts
Thank You for Your sunshine, thank You for Your rain
You paid the ransom for our life You endured our pain

Savior

In times like this we need a Savior
Jesus is one who shows no favor
He is truly an infinite being who died on Calvary for our sins
He cannot lie He cannot steal
You can count on Him, He's real
How precious is His name
He died on Calvary for our shame

Praises

Praises go up, blessings come down
Oh He is worthy, He's yours and mine
Praise Him in the morning
Praise Him in the noonday
Praise Him at night
Just because He's alright
He is an awesome God
He is a Holy God
He is a mighty God
He is worthy to be praised

Pilgrims Traveling Through

Lord, we know we are pilgrims traveling through
On our way to glory to be with You
Lord Help us to be mindful of our journey
Teaching others about you firmly
Teaching them that You are the way
And You are strong enough to keep them from going astray
Letting them know that You are the light
Showing them that Your love is shining bright
By letting Your light shine through us
We will be able to teach them who to trust
Teaching them you are the beginning and the end
Your blood has been shed for their sins
Letting them know you paid it all
All to You we owe
Sin has left a crimson stain
But You can wash them white as snow

Peace

There is peace to be found
Jesus is the answer, He surrounds
He got the whole world in His hands
All we have to do is take a stand
He's alpha and omega the beginning and the end
He's able and willing to wash away our sins
He promise to be with us always
All we have to do is believe in Him and be saved
He is our joy in sorrow
He is our hope for tomorrow
Trust and obey
He will show us the way
Lean not to your own understanding because you will surely stray

No Pain No Gain

David slew Goliath and gained fame
Which nearly drove Saul insane
The undying friendship of Saul's son
Was great gain and also a thorn
David fled to His native country because He was persistently hunted
Because of Saul's jealousy
David soon became a legacy
David endured pain
By the grace of God he gained

Jesus, the Savior of the World

Be not dismayed
Jesus came to save
He came to give us life only if we abide
He said if you abide in Me, and My words abide in you,
you will ask what you desire John 15:7
This is not just for some, but for everyone
Bless His name
He'll never change
He's always the same

Jesus is the Answer

Jesus is the answer for the world today
He is the only one who can show us the way
He is the beginning, He is the end
He came to wash away our sins
He paid the ransom for our life
So we could be with Him in Paradise

I've Been Changed

I've been changed in my Jesus' name
The blood that Jesus shed for me way out on Calvary
He changed my life I am not the same
He picked me up and gave me a new name
Praise Him for His ups, praise Him for His downs
Praise Him for turning me around

Jesus is a Friend

Jesus is a friend
One who will be there to the end
He's the best you will ever know
Because the bible tells us so
He's all wise and all knowing
His love is continually flowing
He is a way maker in times of trouble
Through our ups, even through our struggles
God sent His Son as a ransom for our life
He paid the price with His sacrifice
We cannot repay Him for what He has done
But He tells us to love everyone

Hallelujah

Jesus Christ came to save
Hallelujah is the highest praise
He is the Son of the living God
He is worthy to be praised
He's omnipotent, He's omnipresent,
He's the beginning,
He's the end
He's beyond our greatest imagination,
He died out on Calvary for our sins

Great Is His Name

Great is the name of Jesus
Great is His love for everyone
Great is His power to the powerless
Greatly to be praised
Great is His guidance to guide
Great is His rod and staff to comfort
Great is His ability to save
Greatly to be praised
Great is our God who sent His Son
Great enough to die for everyone
Great authority and honor
Greatly to be praised
Great enough to heal the sick
Great enough to make the blind see
Great enough to raise the dead
Greatly to be praised
Great is His strength and honor
Great enough to endure humility and shame
Great is His reward to those who sustain
Greatly to be praised

God's Love

God's undying love is true
It's not a myth nor is it new
Hold steadfast and let Him speak
He's so gentle and so meek
He's our friend when we are friendless
He's the past present and the future He is endless
He knows all about us from a to z
He knows when we came and when we will leave
He knows us better than we know ourselves
That's the reason we need Him more than anything else

God Sent His Son

God sent His Son
Because He loves everyone
He wants us all to be saved
So the way has been paved
We thank you Lord for saving our souls
From the youngest to the old
You didn't have to do it but you did,
It's so wonderful and we see it
You died out on Calvary for our sins
We know you want us to help bring others in

God Knows All

God knows all
Whether it's big or small
There's nothing He doesn't know
Because the bible tells us so
He's aware of our situations
Our good times and our devastations
Let His rod and staff be our guide
He's standing with outstretched arms saying,
"Come child, come inside"

Earthly Vessels

We are earthly vessels of the Lord
He gave us a new start
He opened His arms for us to come in
We believed and confessed our sins
It lets us know He cares for us
All He wants is our complete trust
Now we are heirs and joint heirs to the thrown
Praise you Lord, You sent Your Son for our wrongs

Fix It Jesus

Whatever the problem may be
The bible has the answer, read it and see
He fixed it for Paul
And that's not all
He fixed it for Daniel
Just like He fixed it for Samuel
He can fix it for youth
Just like He did it for Ruth
He can fix it for old
Just like He did it for Job
He fixed it for Joseph
Just like He did it for Moses
He can fix it for you
Because God's word is the truth

Faith

Faith is reliance on Jesus Christ
when you accept Him watch Him smile
You may be sinking in the deepest of sin
But Jesus stands with outstretched arms saying come,
my child, come on in
Repent your heart and be godly sorry you don't have to
wait until tomorrow
Unless you repent, you will perish
Please don't wait, don't tarry
Let not your hearts be troubled
The blood of Jesus was shed to cover
He is the one and only God
Relax and give Him your heart

Come to Jesus

Come to Jesus as you are He is a bright and morning star
He will wipe away all tears He has done this for many years
It doesn't matter how long you've lived just believe
and you are sealed
He came to save our souls you can be young or old
He stands with outstretched arms there to protect us from all harm

Victorious

We were in fact Notorious sinners
Our belief in Jesus made us Victorious winners
We were headed for destruction
Jesus death on Calvary was a major interruption
He paid the ransom on our account
He was not concern about the amount
He loved us very much, it's true
He only ask we trust and obey
That's all He wants from me and you

Walk Worthy

Walk worthy of your call
Just remember Jesus has paid it all
We can never pay Him back
Just stay focused and stay on track
He leads us and guides us every step of the way
If His word abides in us and we abide in Him,
we will not go astray
Give Him praise for what He has done, is doing, and will do
Trust Him, obey Him, He will see you through

True Love

Jesus' loving care puts our mind at ease
So we can surely have peace
A close relationship totally depending on God
Means to a sinner we are very odd
If we love God with all our Heart
We must believe Jesus is the Son of God
Love hides multitudes of faults
Of the earth, we are the salt
Love went to Calvary for our sins
So each of us has an opportunity to be cleansed

Undying Love

God's undying love is true
It's not a myth nor is it new
Hold steadfast and let Him speak
He's so gentle and so meek
Yes He loves us true enough
But we must humble ourselves and trust
Love is what the world needs
Trust Him and you will succeed
Beyond a shadow of a doubt
I guarantee He will work it out
You see I have tried Him and I know
Blessed be His name He loves us so

Survivor

Marriage is two people bonded until death do they part
So you should think of this even before you start
Jesus said I am the groom and you are the bride
All we have to do is open the door and let Him step inside
There's no part A nor part B
One thing fits all for you and for me
Jesus said come to me, all you who labor and are heavy laden
and I will give you rest Matt. 11:28
Are you sure you are ready for the test?
It's not that you should score a hundred on the test
Just start with love and Jesus will do the rest
He said if you abide in me and my word abide in you
Ask anything in my name and it shall be done
Because of our sinful nature God has sent His Son
Trust in Him without a doubt
I guarantee you God will bring you out
You can survive
With Jesus on your side

Seek and Ye Shall Find

Seek the Lord and you will find
He is omnipotent, He is divine
Come to Him just as you are
He's the bright and morning star
Trust Him in all your ways
Then shout His name and give Him praise

Redeem

With Christ's death on the cross
He paid the price to release us all
From the bondage of our sins
With this act satan can't win
He freed us from damnation of sin
So we can produce good works and glorify Him
We are to resist the evil of the world
Trust Jesus, only Him we must serve

Prayer

Prayer is merely a conversation with God
Even if there are so many complications and odds
Those that do not know Him in the pardon of your sins
I want you to know you can be washed and cleansed
Come to Jesus just as you are
With a repentant heart by far
Your remorse God does detect
He is all powerful and He will not reject
Believe Jesus is the Son of the living God
He died and rose for our hearts
Give your heart to Jesus and be at peace
Know all of your troubles will not cease
But He said come unto Him
All ye that labor and are heavy laden
And He will give you rest
So you see, Jesus is the very best

POWER

THERE IS POWER IN Jesus name
When you confess your faults and believe in Him you're not the same
He gives you a new start
Simple because He changes your heart
You are a new creature in Christ
Jesus went to Calvary and sacrificed
He paid the ransom and pardoned your sin
He washed and cleansed you from within
There is power in Jesus name
Your purpose in life has changed

Not My Will Lord

When you subject your mind and will
To Jesus' will, you shall be filled
Knowing God in the pardon of your sins
Makes it confusing to those that don't know Him
God being the infinite being that He is
Should give us a more zealous zeal
Oh what Jesus went through for us
He was battered and scorned to win our trust
God is our maker and creator
He sent His Son Jesus Christ to save us

Mother's Love

Remembering the love my mother had for me
Didn't understand it then, but now I see
Chastised me when I did wrong
Which later made me strong
She rewarded me for my good
That part I understood
It let me know I had to take the bitter with the sweet
We as God's children, this is what makes us so unique

Meditate

Meditate day and night
David did it, He was alright
He was a man after God's own heart
This is where it all did start
He said and I will meditate in thy statutes Psalm119:48B
Because none other is more righteous
If we meditate daily on His word
When trials come we will not be disturbed
Trust God and obey
There's no better way

Lord Over Long Term Illness

There was a woman that had an issue of blood
She suffered long, but then she was heard
She spent everything she had in hope of being cured
But the disorder of blood lasted twelve long years
One day she heard Jesus was in the area
With her faith she knew He would take care of her
So she joined the crowd that followed Jesus
She touched the hem of His garment and was healed immediately
Oh what a mighty God we serve
Our moans, our groans, our cry He heard
Now faith is the substance of things hoped for
The evidence of things not seen Hebrew 11:4

Led by the Spirit of God

God's spirit will lead us through
Whatever it is we need to do
He is our provider, our protector
He is our director
He's God almighty all by Himself
He don't need any help from anyone else
He's the Creator of the universe
He's the beginning, He is the first
There's none other before Him
There's none other like Him
He's the source of our being
He loved us so much He sent His only begotten
Son to die for our sins

I Worship Thee Lord

Lord, I worship you for who you are
You are my bright and morning star
You are the Savior of the world
There's none other worthy to serve
You hung, bled and died for me
Lord I pray you keep me close to thee
I worship you for opening my eyes
I worship you for being my guide

How Precious is His Name

How precious is the name of Jesus
He is the Son of God who sees us
Everything we say or do
So you see, He knows us through and through
He is the holy one of God
There is no problem He can't solve
He intercedes on our behalf
He has done this in ages past
He is our hope for years to come
This is for everyone, not just for some
So let us lift our head in praise
And recognize He is the one who saves

Grace and Mercy

Sin had us bound
But Grace says, loose them, put them down
Mercy says I will not forsake them
My love extends beyond and I pardon their sin
Satan thought He had us
But Grace and Mercy reached down and saved us
Thank God for His grace and mercy
Without him we still would be searching

A Gift

Children are a gift from God
Even when they act like snobs
Raise them in the fear of God
They will not depart

God Created Man

God created man
Men, you have got to take a stand
He said I give you a wife
Just to be by your side
Love her and give her respect
This is all I expect
Church, I am the groom
And you are the bride
I bid you to obey me
And I will abide
Lean not on your own understanding
But look to me I am not very demanding
All I ask is that you have
The faith of a mustard seed
And when that time comes
You will be with me indeed

Elderly

The elderly in society today
Seem as though they are in the way
There is a saying, "once an adult twice a child"
But if we live on, we will be there after a while
From the womb to the grave
There is for some a lot of space
It doesn't matter about how many days
Just as long as you are saved

So there is nothing physically left after that but dust
So you see, our bodies won't live forever physically
But if we live for Christ forever, we will spiritually
We will have eternal life with Christ in Heaven
We can have that even if we accept Him at age eleven
So all it takes is denying ourselves
Follow Jesus and no one else

Dear Lord

Dear Lord hear our cry
Please Jesus, don't pass us by
Our hearts are heavy, our eyes are full of tears
We are crying out to you because we know you are real
So much trouble in the world today
Please Lord hear us when we pray
You said cast our burdens upon you and you shall sustain us
In thee, we know you are able Lord, we have just got to trust
Oh Lord, look down upon us cast out all fears and doubts
Help us to know you're able to get us ready to shout
Precious Lord, take our hand
Lead us on help us to stand

Celebrate!!!

Come let us celebrate
Jesus saved our souls and it wasn't too late
He came, He died and He rose
He died for the young as well as the old
He came once to save our souls
He'll be back to carry us with Him
Where the street is paved with gold
Jesus is great
Come let us celebrate!!!

Building God's kingdom

Let us build God's kingdom with the tools that He gave
Bestowing upon others the fact that He saves
Your gifts are the tools to success
If used in the manner that they were given
We are blessed
Glory to His name, Jesus is always the same
He died out on Calvary in order for us to make a change
It's our choice to receive Him, He doesn't push nor does He pull
But when we subject our mind and our will to the very essence of
His will we will be filled
Praise is what I do because God is so true
Hallelujah is the highest praise He allowed us to do
God being the infinite being that He is
Should give us a zealous zeal
Especially when we witness to others that He lives
You're going to be talked about as sure you are born
But look at Jesus He was battered and scorned
Oh what Jesus went through for us beaten and scorned
For all that trust, let us lift our hands in praise
And let the world know He still saves

Our Time is of Essence

It's important how we spend our time
should we stay focus and keep Jesus in mine
We as christians we depend on our savior
communication with him keep us stable
God is love and he demonstrated it in the gift of his son
He hung his head bleed and died for everyone
In worship we know what is of highest worth
not ourselves others not even our works
The greatest desire of God is that we love him with our whole being
praise and give him thanks for washing away our sins

www.ingramcontent.com/pod-product-compliance
Ingram Content Group UK Ltd.
Pitfield, Milton Keynes, MK11 3LW, UK
UKHW022220230426
12048UKWH00016BA/957